MY FISH LOG BOOK

THIS BOOK BELONGS TO:

_____

_____

_____

FISHING LOG

LOCATION:	DATE:
FISHING WITH:	
START TIME:	END TIME:

WEATHER:

MOON PHASE:

TIME	SPECIES	BAIT	WEIGHT	LENGTH

NOTES:

A PHOTO OR SKETCH FROM THIS FISHING TRIP

THIS FISHING TRIP RATING

☆ ☆ ☆ ☆ ☆

FISHING LOG

LOCATION:	DATE:
FISHING WITH:	
START TIME:	END TIME:

WEATHER:

MOON PHASE:

TIME	SPECIES	BAIT	WEIGHT	LENGTH

NOTES:

A PHOTO OR SKETCH FROM THIS FISHING TRIP

THIS FISHING TRIP RATING

FISHING LOG

LOCATION:	DATE:
FISHING WITH:	
START TIME:	END TIME:

WEATHER:

MOON PHASE:

TIME	SPECIES	BAIT	WEIGHT	LENGTH

NOTES:

A PHOTO OR SKETCH FROM THIS FISHING TRIP

THIS FISHING TRIP RATING

☆ ☆ ☆ ☆ ☆

FISHING LOG

LOCATION: on a brig	DATE:
FISHING WITH: baber	
START TIME:	END TIME:

WEATHER:

MOON PHASE:

TIME	SPECIES	BAIT	WEIGHT	LENGTH
	gike	liv fish		90cm
	gherch	magets		
		minozo		

NOTES:

A PHOTO OR SKETCH FROM THIS FISHING TRIP

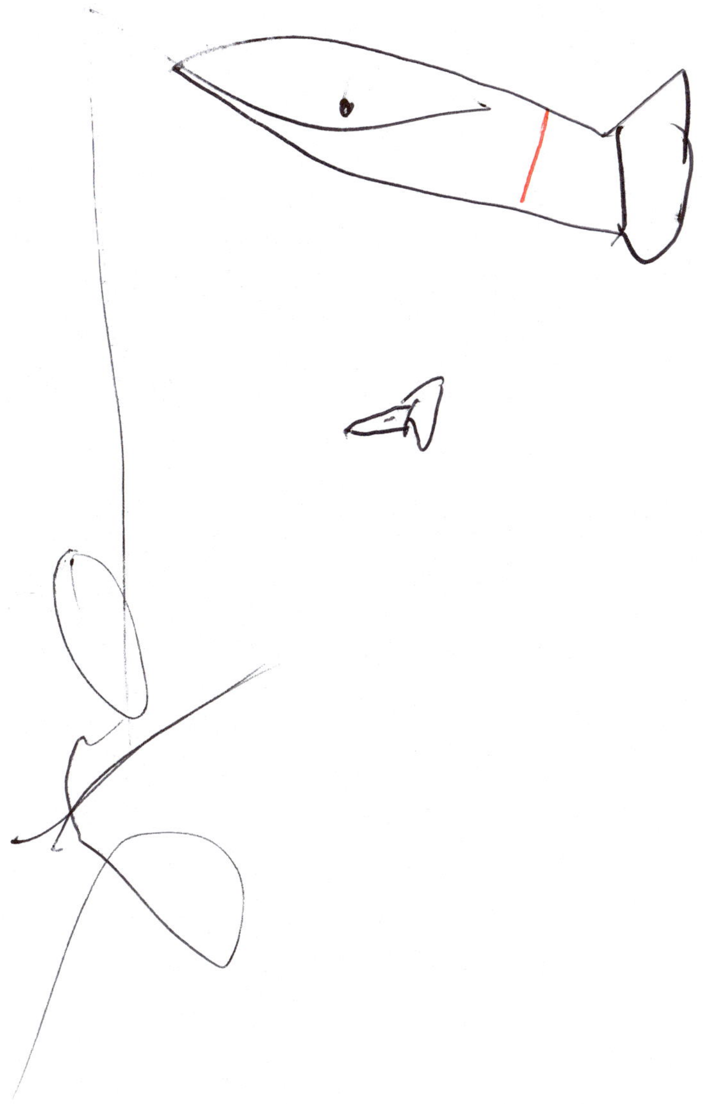

THIS FISHING TRIP RATING

FISHING LOG

LOCATION:	DATE:
FISHING WITH:	
START TIME:	END TIME:

WEATHER:

MOON PHASE:

TIME	SPECIES	BAIT	WEIGHT	LENGTH

NOTES:

A PHOTO OR SKETCH FROM THIS FISHING TRIP

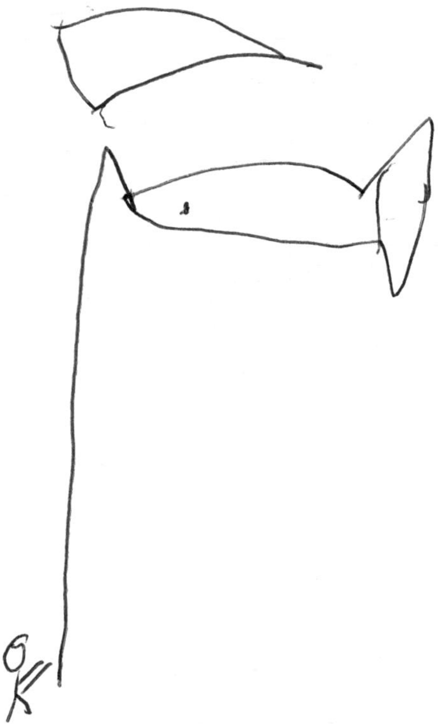

THIS FISHING TRIP RATING

FISHING LOG

LOCATION:	DATE:
FISHING WITH:	
START TIME:	END TIME:

WEATHER: all or ren

MOON PHASE:

TIME	SPECIES	BAIT	WEIGHT	LENGTH
Th				

NOTES:

A PHOTO OR SKETCH FROM THIS FISHING TRIP

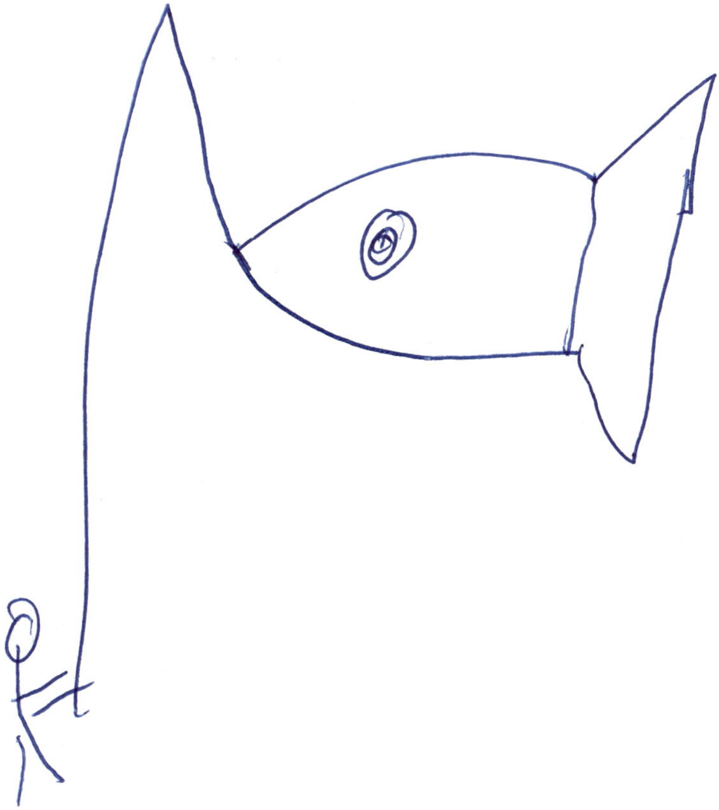

THIS FISHING TRIP RATING

FISHING LOG

LOCATION:	DATE:
FISHING WITH:	
START TIME:	END TIME:

WEATHER:

MOON PHASE:

TIME	SPECIES	BAIT	WEIGHT	LENGTH
9o'clock		fish Wurmse		
	8+8000			
		8+8000		

NOTES:

800

A PHOTO OR SKETCH FROM THIS FISHING TRIP

puroh

THIS FISHING TRIP RATING

FISHING LOG

LOCATION:	DATE:
FISHING WITH:	
START TIME:	END TIME:

WEATHER:

MOON PHASE:

TIME	SPECIES	BAIT	WEIGHT	LENGTH

NOTES:

A PHOTO OR SKETCH FROM THIS FISHING TRIP

THIS FISHING TRIP RATING

FISHING LOG

LOCATION:	DATE:
FISHING WITH:	
START TIME:	END TIME:

WEATHER:

☐ ☐ ☐ ☐ ☐

MOON PHASE:

☐ ☐ ☐ ☐ ☐ ☐ ☐ ☐

TIME	SPECIES	BAIT	WEIGHT	LENGTH

NOTES:

A PHOTO OR SKETCH FROM THIS FISHING TRIP

THIS FISHING TRIP RATING
☆ ☆ ☆ ☆ ☆

FISHING LOG

LOCATION:	DATE:
FISHING WITH:	
START TIME:	END TIME:

WEATHER:

MOON PHASE:

TIME	SPECIES	BAIT	WEIGHT	LENGTH

NOTES:

FISHING LOG

LOCATION:	DATE:
FISHING WITH:	
START TIME:	END TIME:

WEATHER:

MOON PHASE:

TIME	SPECIES	BAIT	WEIGHT	LENGTH

NOTES:

A PHOTO OR SKETCH FROM THIS FISHING TRIP

THIS FISHING TRIP RATING

☆ ☆ ☆ ☆ ☆

FISHING LOG

LOCATION:	DATE:
FISHING WITH:	
START TIME:	END TIME:

WEATHER:

MOON PHASE:

TIME	SPECIES	BAIT	WEIGHT	LENGTH

NOTES:

FISHING LOG

LOCATION:	DATE:
FISHING WITH:	
START TIME:	END TIME:

WEATHER:

☐ ☐ ☐ ☐ ☐

MOON PHASE:

☐ ☐ ☐ ☐ ☐ ☐ ☐ ☐

TIME	SPECIES	BAIT	WEIGHT	LENGTH

NOTES:

A PHOTO OR SKETCH FROM THIS FISHING TRIP

THIS FISHING TRIP RATING

FISHING LOG

LOCATION:	DATE:
FISHING WITH:	
START TIME:	END TIME:

WEATHER:

MOON PHASE:

TIME	SPECIES	BAIT	WEIGHT	LENGTH

NOTES:

A PHOTO OR SKETCH FROM THIS FISHING TRIP

THIS FISHING TRIP RATING

FISHING LOG

LOCATION:	DATE:
FISHING WITH:	
START TIME:	END TIME:

WEATHER:

MOON PHASE:

TIME	SPECIES	BAIT	WEIGHT	LENGTH

NOTES:

FISHING LOG

LOCATION:	DATE:
FISHING WITH:	
START TIME:	END TIME:

WEATHER:

MOON PHASE:

TIME	SPECIES	BAIT	WEIGHT	LENGTH

NOTES:

A PHOTO OR SKETCH FROM THIS FISHING TRIP

THIS FISHING TRIP RATING

FISHING LOG

LOCATION:	DATE:
FISHING WITH:	
START TIME:	END TIME:

WEATHER:

☐ ☐ ☐ ☐ ☐

MOON PHASE:

☐ ☐ ☐ ☐ ☐ ☐ ☐ ☐ ☐

TIME	SPECIES	BAIT	WEIGHT	LENGTH

NOTES:

A PHOTO OR SKETCH FROM THIS FISHING TRIP

THIS FISHING TRIP RATING

☆ ☆ ☆ ☆ ☆

FISHING LOG

LOCATION:	DATE:
FISHING WITH:	
START TIME:	END TIME:

WEATHER:

☐ ☐ ☐ ☐ ☐

MOON PHASE:

☐ ☐ ☐ ☐ ☐ ☐ ☐ ☐

TIME	SPECIES	BAIT	WEIGHT	LENGTH

NOTES:

A PHOTO OR SKETCH FROM THIS FISHING TRIP

THIS FISHING TRIP RATING
☆ ☆ ☆ ☆ ☆

FISHING LOG

LOCATION:	DATE:
FISHING WITH:	
START TIME:	END TIME:

WEATHER:

☀ ☐ ⛅ ☐ 🌧 ☐ ⛈ ☐ ❄ ☐

MOON PHASE:

☐ ☐ ☐ ☐ ☐ ☐ ☐ ☐ ☐

TIME	SPECIES	BAIT	WEIGHT	LENGTH

NOTES:

A PHOTO OR SKETCH FROM THIS FISHING TRIP

THIS FISHING TRIP RATING

☆ ☆ ☆ ☆ ☆

FISHING LOG

LOCATION:	DATE:
FISHING WITH:	
START TIME:	END TIME:

WEATHER:

MOON PHASE:

TIME	SPECIES	BAIT	WEIGHT	LENGTH

NOTES:

A PHOTO OR SKETCH FROM THIS FISHING TRIP

THIS FISHING TRIP RATING
☆ ☆ ☆ ☆ ☆

FISHING LOG

LOCATION:	DATE:
FISHING WITH:	
START TIME:	END TIME:

WEATHER:

MOON PHASE:

TIME	SPECIES	BAIT	WEIGHT	LENGTH

NOTES:

A PHOTO OR SKETCH FROM THIS FISHING TRIP

THIS FISHING TRIP RATING

☆ ☆ ☆ ☆ ☆

FISHING LOG

LOCATION:	DATE:
FISHING WITH:	
START TIME:	END TIME:

WEATHER:

☀️ ☐ ⛅ ☐ 🌧️ ☐ ⛈️ ☐ ❄️ ☐

MOON PHASE:

☐ ☐ ☐ ☐ ☐ ☐ ☐ ☐ ☐

TIME	SPECIES	BAIT	WEIGHT	LENGTH

NOTES:

A PHOTO OR SKETCH FROM THIS FISHING TRIP

THIS FISHING TRIP RATING

☆ ☆ ☆ ☆ ☆

FISHING LOG

LOCATION:	DATE:
FISHING WITH:	
START TIME:	END TIME:

WEATHER:

MOON PHASE:

TIME	SPECIES	BAIT	WEIGHT	LENGTH

NOTES:

A PHOTO OR SKETCH FROM THIS FISHING TRIP

THIS FISHING TRIP RATING

☆ ☆ ☆ ☆ ☆

FISHING LOG

LOCATION:	DATE:
FISHING WITH:	
START TIME:	END TIME:

WEATHER:

MOON PHASE:

TIME	SPECIES	BAIT	WEIGHT	LENGTH

NOTES:

A PHOTO OR SKETCH FROM THIS FISHING TRIP

THIS FISHING TRIP RATING

☆ ☆ ☆ ☆ ☆

FISHING LOG

LOCATION:	DATE:
FISHING WITH:	
START TIME:	END TIME:

WEATHER:

MOON PHASE:

TIME	SPECIES	BAIT	WEIGHT	LENGTH

NOTES:

A PHOTO OR SKETCH FROM THIS FISHING TRIP

THIS FISHING TRIP RATING
☆ ☆ ☆ ☆ ☆

FISHING LOG

LOCATION:	DATE:
FISHING WITH:	
START TIME:	END TIME:

WEATHER:

MOON PHASE:

TIME	SPECIES	BAIT	WEIGHT	LENGTH

NOTES:

A PHOTO OR SKETCH FROM THIS FISHING TRIP

THIS FISHING TRIP RATING

☆ ☆ ☆ ☆ ☆

FISHING LOG

LOCATION:	DATE:
FISHING WITH:	
START TIME:	END TIME:

WEATHER:

MOON PHASE:

TIME	SPECIES	BAIT	WEIGHT	LENGTH

NOTES:

A PHOTO OR SKETCH FROM THIS FISHING TRIP

THIS FISHING TRIP RATING

☆ ☆ ☆ ☆ ☆

FISHING LOG

LOCATION:	DATE:
FISHING WITH:	
START TIME:	END TIME:

WEATHER:

☐ Sunny ☐ Partly Cloudy ☐ Rainy ☐ Stormy ☐ Snowy

MOON PHASE:

☐ ☐ ☐ ☐ ☐ ☐ ☐ ☐

TIME	SPECIES	BAIT	WEIGHT	LENGTH

NOTES:

A PHOTO OR SKETCH FROM THIS FISHING TRIP

THIS FISHING TRIP RATING

☆ ☆ ☆ ☆ ☆

FISHING LOG

LOCATION:	DATE:
FISHING WITH:	
START TIME:	END TIME:

WEATHER:

☐ Sunny ☐ Partly Cloudy ☐ Rainy ☐ Stormy ☐ Snowy

MOON PHASE:

☐ ☐ ☐ ☐ ☐ ☐ ☐ ☐

TIME	SPECIES	BAIT	WEIGHT	LENGTH

NOTES:

A PHOTO OR SKETCH FROM THIS FISHING TRIP

THIS FISHING TRIP RATING

☆ ☆ ☆ ☆ ☆

FISHING LOG

LOCATION:	DATE:
FISHING WITH:	
START TIME:	END TIME:

WEATHER:

MOON PHASE:

TIME	SPECIES	BAIT	WEIGHT	LENGTH

NOTES:

A PHOTO OR SKETCH FROM THIS FISHING TRIP

THIS FISHING TRIP RATING

☆ ☆ ☆ ☆ ☆

FISHING LOG

LOCATION:	DATE:
FISHING WITH:	
START TIME:	END TIME:

WEATHER:

MOON PHASE:

TIME	SPECIES	BAIT	WEIGHT	LENGTH

NOTES:

A PHOTO OR SKETCH FROM THIS FISHING TRIP

THIS FISHING TRIP RATING
☆ ☆ ☆ ☆ ☆

FISHING LOG

LOCATION:	DATE:
FISHING WITH:	
START TIME:	END TIME:

WEATHER:

MOON PHASE:

TIME	SPECIES	BAIT	WEIGHT	LENGTH

NOTES:

A PHOTO OR SKETCH FROM THIS FISHING TRIP

THIS FISHING TRIP RATING

☆ ☆ ☆ ☆ ☆

FISHING LOG

LOCATION:	DATE:
FISHING WITH:	
START TIME:	END TIME:

WEATHER:

☐ Sunny ☐ Partly Cloudy ☐ Rainy ☐ Thunderstorm ☐ Snow

MOON PHASE:

☐ ☐ ☐ ☐ ☐ ☐ ☐ ☐

TIME	SPECIES	BAIT	WEIGHT	LENGTH

NOTES:

A PHOTO OR SKETCH FROM THIS FISHING TRIP

THIS FISHING TRIP RATING

☆ ☆ ☆ ☆ ☆

FISHING LOG

LOCATION:	DATE:
FISHING WITH:	
START TIME:	END TIME:

WEATHER:

MOON PHASE:

TIME	SPECIES	BAIT	WEIGHT	LENGTH

NOTES:

A PHOTO OR SKETCH FROM THIS FISHING TRIP

THIS FISHING TRIP RATING

☆ ☆ ☆ ☆ ☆

FISHING LOG

LOCATION:	DATE:
FISHING WITH:	
START TIME:	END TIME:

WEATHER:

MOON PHASE:

TIME	SPECIES	BAIT	WEIGHT	LENGTH

NOTES:

A PHOTO OR SKETCH FROM THIS FISHING TRIP

THIS FISHING TRIP RATING
☆ ☆ ☆ ☆ ☆

FISHING LOG

LOCATION:	DATE:
FISHING WITH:	
START TIME:	END TIME:

WEATHER:

MOON PHASE:

TIME	SPECIES	BAIT	WEIGHT	LENGTH

NOTES:

A PHOTO OR SKETCH FROM THIS FISHING TRIP

THIS FISHING TRIP RATING
☆ ☆ ☆ ☆ ☆

FISHING LOG

LOCATION:	DATE:
FISHING WITH:	
START TIME:	END TIME:

WEATHER:

MOON PHASE:

TIME	SPECIES	BAIT	WEIGHT	LENGTH

NOTES:

A PHOTO OR SKETCH FROM THIS FISHING TRIP

THIS FISHING TRIP RATING

☆ ☆ ☆ ☆ ☆

FISHING LOG

LOCATION:	DATE:
FISHING WITH:	
START TIME:	END TIME:

WEATHER:

MOON PHASE:

TIME	SPECIES	BAIT	WEIGHT	LENGTH

NOTES:

A PHOTO OR SKETCH FROM THIS FISHING TRIP

THIS FISHING TRIP RATING

☆ ☆ ☆ ☆ ☆

FISHING LOG

LOCATION:	DATE:
FISHING WITH:	
START TIME:	END TIME:

WEATHER:

MOON PHASE:

TIME	SPECIES	BAIT	WEIGHT	LENGTH

NOTES:

A PHOTO OR SKETCH FROM THIS FISHING TRIP

THIS FISHING TRIP RATING

☆ ☆ ☆ ☆ ☆

FISHING LOG

LOCATION:	DATE:
FISHING WITH:	
START TIME:	END TIME:

WEATHER:

MOON PHASE:

TIME	SPECIES	BAIT	WEIGHT	LENGTH

NOTES:

A PHOTO OR SKETCH FROM THIS FISHING TRIP

THIS FISHING TRIP RATING
☆ ☆ ☆ ☆ ☆

FISHING LOG

LOCATION:	DATE:
FISHING WITH:	
START TIME:	END TIME:

WEATHER:

☀️ ⛅ 🌧️ ⛈️ ❄️

MOON PHASE:

TIME	SPECIES	BAIT	WEIGHT	LENGTH

NOTES:

A PHOTO OR SKETCH FROM THIS FISHING TRIP

THIS FISHING TRIP RATING

☆ ☆ ☆ ☆ ☆

FISHING LOG

LOCATION:	DATE:
FISHING WITH:	
START TIME:	END TIME:

WEATHER:

MOON PHASE:

TIME	SPECIES	BAIT	WEIGHT	LENGTH

NOTES:

A PHOTO OR SKETCH FROM THIS FISHING TRIP

THIS FISHING TRIP RATING

☆ ☆ ☆ ☆ ☆

FISHING LOG

LOCATION:	DATE:
FISHING WITH:	
START TIME:	END TIME:

WEATHER:

MOON PHASE:

TIME	SPECIES	BAIT	WEIGHT	LENGTH

NOTES:

A PHOTO OR SKETCH FROM THIS FISHING TRIP

THIS FISHING TRIP RATING

☆ ☆ ☆ ☆ ☆

FISHING LOG

LOCATION:	DATE:
FISHING WITH:	
START TIME:	END TIME:

WEATHER:

☀ ☐   ⛅ ☐   🌧 ☐   ⛈ ☐   ❄ ☐

MOON PHASE:

☐ ☐ ☐ ☐ ☐ ☐ ☐ ☐

TIME	SPECIES	BAIT	WEIGHT	LENGTH

NOTES:

A PHOTO OR SKETCH FROM THIS FISHING TRIP

THIS FISHING TRIP RATING

☆ ☆ ☆ ☆ ☆

FISHING LOG

LOCATION:	DATE:
FISHING WITH:	
START TIME:	END TIME:

WEATHER:

☐ Sunny ☐ Partly Cloudy ☐ Rainy ☐ Stormy ☐ Snowy

MOON PHASE:

☐ ☐ ☐ ☐ ☐ ☐ ☐ ☐

TIME	SPECIES	BAIT	WEIGHT	LENGTH

NOTES:

A PHOTO OR SKETCH FROM THIS FISHING TRIP

THIS FISHING TRIP RATING

☆ ☆ ☆ ☆ ☆

FISHING LOG

LOCATION:	DATE:
FISHING WITH:	
START TIME:	END TIME:

WEATHER:

MOON PHASE:

TIME	SPECIES	BAIT	WEIGHT	LENGTH

NOTES:

A PHOTO OR SKETCH FROM THIS FISHING TRIP

THIS FISHING TRIP RATING

☆ ☆ ☆ ☆ ☆

FISHING LOG

LOCATION:	DATE:
FISHING WITH:	
START TIME:	END TIME:

WEATHER:

☐ ☐ ☐ ☐ ☐

MOON PHASE:

☐ ☐ ☐ ☐ ☐ ☐ ☐ ☐

TIME	SPECIES	BAIT	WEIGHT	LENGTH

NOTES:

A PHOTO OR SKETCH FROM THIS FISHING TRIP

THIS FISHING TRIP RATING

☆ ☆ ☆ ☆ ☆

FISHING LOG

LOCATION:		DATE:	
FISHING WITH:			
START TIME:		END TIME:	

WEATHER:

MOON PHASE:

TIME	SPECIES	BAIT	WEIGHT	LENGTH

NOTES:

A PHOTO OR SKETCH FROM THIS FISHING TRIP

THIS FISHING TRIP RATING

☆ ☆ ☆ ☆ ☆

FISHING LOG

LOCATION:	DATE:
FISHING WITH:	
START TIME:	END TIME:

WEATHER:

MOON PHASE:

TIME	SPECIES	BAIT	WEIGHT	LENGTH

NOTES:

A PHOTO OR SKETCH FROM THIS FISHING TRIP

THIS FISHING TRIP RATING

☆ ☆ ☆ ☆ ☆

FISHING LOG

LOCATION:	DATE:
FISHING WITH:	
START TIME:	END TIME:

WEATHER:

☐ Sunny ☐ Partly Cloudy ☐ Rainy ☐ Stormy ☐ Snowy

MOON PHASE:

☐ ☐ ☐ ☐ ☐ ☐ ☐ ☐ ☐

TIME	SPECIES	BAIT	WEIGHT	LENGTH

NOTES:

A PHOTO OR SKETCH FROM THIS FISHING TRIP

THIS FISHING TRIP RATING
☆ ☆ ☆ ☆ ☆

FISHING LOG

LOCATION:	DATE:
FISHING WITH:	
START TIME:	END TIME:

WEATHER:

MOON PHASE:

TIME	SPECIES	BAIT	WEIGHT	LENGTH

NOTES:

A PHOTO OR SKETCH FROM THIS FISHING TRIP

THIS FISHING TRIP RATING

☆ ☆ ☆ ☆ ☆

FISHING LOG

LOCATION:	DATE:
FISHING WITH:	
START TIME:	END TIME:

WEATHER:

☀️ ☁️ 🌧️ ⛈️ ❄️

MOON PHASE:

🌑 🌒 🌓 🌔 🌕 🌖 🌗 🌘 🌒

TIME	SPECIES	BAIT	WEIGHT	LENGTH

NOTES:

A PHOTO OR SKETCH FROM THIS FISHING TRIP

THIS FISHING TRIP RATING

☆ ☆ ☆ ☆ ☆

FISHING LOG

LOCATION:	DATE:
FISHING WITH:	
START TIME:	END TIME:

WEATHER:

MOON PHASE:

TIME	SPECIES	BAIT	WEIGHT	LENGTH

NOTES:

A PHOTO OR SKETCH FROM THIS FISHING TRIP

THIS FISHING TRIP RATING

☆ ☆ ☆ ☆ ☆

FISHING LOG

LOCATION:	DATE:
FISHING WITH:	
START TIME:	END TIME:

WEATHER:

MOON PHASE:

TIME	SPECIES	BAIT	WEIGHT	LENGTH

NOTES:

A PHOTO OR SKETCH FROM THIS FISHING TRIP

THIS FISHING TRIP RATING
☆ ☆ ☆ ☆ ☆

FISHING LOG

LOCATION:	DATE:
FISHING WITH:	
START TIME:	END TIME:

WEATHER:

☀️ ☐   ⛅ ☐   🌧️ ☐   ⛈️ ☐   ❄️ ☐

MOON PHASE:

☐ ☐ ☐ ☐ ☐ ☐ ☐ ☐ ☐

TIME	SPECIES	BAIT	WEIGHT	LENGTH

NOTES:

A PHOTO OR SKETCH FROM THIS FISHING TRIP

THIS FISHING TRIP RATING

☆ ☆ ☆ ☆ ☆

Printed in Great Britain
by Amazon